THE PITT RIVERS MUSEUM

by Julia Cousins

As David Attenborough says in his foreword, the Pitt Rivers Museum is unique. Unsuspecting visitors walking into the main court of the museum often have little idea of what awaits them. The sheer volume of material competing for their attention and the richness of the mixture is overwhelming. Treasures are displayed not only in cases, but hanging from the ceiling and cramming every inch of available space. This does make considerable demands on the visitor, who is challenged to find a way of responding to the museum's visual and imaginative impact. Perhaps it is best simply to experience it and let the museum find its own way of communicating to you.

But sooner or later the questions begin to arise. Why is it called Pitt Rivers? Why is it arranged as it is? What goes on behind the scenes? This booklet is designed to answer some of these questions and to help the visitor understand what makes the museum so special and so different.

The story begins, of course, with General Pitt Rivers, but the museum today owes as much, if not more, to two other people, Henry Balfour and Beatrice Blackwood. All three were innovators and largely self-taught, for they were at the very beginnings of the modern development of archaeology and anthropology. Their great strength lay in embracing a wide range of diverse interests and material and they were among those who laid the foundations of the more specialised modern disciplines. The Pitt Rivers Museum has played a significant part in the academic development of these subjects and one has always to remember that it is a university teaching collection as well as a museum of international renown.

Who was Pitt Rivers?

General Pitt Rivers, as he is now always known, was born Augustus Henry Lane Fox in 1827. He was required to take the name Pitt Rivers when he eventually succeeded to the Cranborne Estates. Like so many second sons of second sons at that time, he was destined for a military career. At eighteen he was commissioned in the Grenadier Guards, having acquired the skills in mathematics, model-making, technical drawing and surveying necessary to an army officer, all of which would be used to such advantage in his later archaeological work.

Although he rose to be a Lieutenant-General by the time he retired in 1882, had seen distinguished active service in the Crimean War in 1854 and had various postings abroad, his military career was really to be the background to his other achievements.

His first duties in London seem to have been mainly administrative and ceremonial, not demanding enough for an energetic and serious-minded young man. However, they brought him into contact with the Stanley family whose wide circle of intellectual and political friends gave direction to his hunger for intellectual self-improvement. He also fell in love with Alice Stanley, who was later to become his wife and by whom he had nine children.

In 1850 Pitt Rivers was given a routine assignment to help with the testing of the new Minié rifle. He was involved in making some modifications to it and wrote the drill manual for its use. The unexpected result was that he became passionately interested in the historical development of firearms and, by extension, of other objects. In about 1851 he began to make a personal collection. He started with firearms and weaponry but rapidly became an omnivorous collector.

Outside events were also to play their part in the development both of his collection and of his theories about it. The Great Exhibition of 1851 had

From the displays of clubs and other weapons in the Upper Gallery. 'Offensive and defensive' weaponry was the General's first interest and the museum has a remarkable collection.

encapsulated the Victorian ideas of the march of progress from the simple and primitive to the more sophisticated and civilised. In 1859 Darwin's *Origin of Species* was published. This was undoubtedly the spur to Pitt Rivers' belief that there could be a systematic classification and

Model boats in the Court, many from the original Pitt Rivers collection.

Photograph: John Reader.

arrangement of material objects which would reveal the course of the evolution of human culture. In other words, objects were to be classified like biological species and Pitt Rivers invented the word 'typology' to describe this arrangement in sequences of forms.

'Progress', he wrote in his lecture on the Evolution of Culture, 'is like a game of dominoes – like fits on to like. In neither case can we tell beforehand what will be the ultimate figure produced by the adhesions; all we know is that the fundamental rule of the game is sequence'. There would be found, he was convinced, a 'predictable course of gradual improvements' in the evolution of any material object from its earliest beginnings to its most sophisticated form.

The Victorians saw the pursuit of Scientific Truth almost as a religion in itself. The United Services Institution, and societies such as the Geographical, the Ethnological and later the Anthropological, all encouraged lectures and debate and the making of scientific collections. Pitt Rivers was to be associated with them all and to take a leading role in their affairs. Through them he met travellers such as Richard Burton and Sir John Petherick, army and navy officers returning from various parts of the British Empire with all sorts of intriguing mementoes and scientists such as T. H. Huxley. The great Darwinian biologist's famous debate with Bishop Wilberforce of Oxford took place just next door in the University Museum.

The 1860s were the most important period in the development of Pitt Rivers' collection. His colleagues and professional contacts brought him material; he also purchased extensively, if selectively, from dealers, choosing individual pieces which would fill the gaps in his evolutionary sequences. His aim was to fill in the historical continuum, 'the living scroll of human progress', realizing the direct relationship between the simple technology of modern native peoples and our own archaeological past. It was 'the commoner type of object' which interested him; 'the ordinary and typical specimens' not the rare and exotic which would only have curiosity value.

By the end of the 1860s Pitt Rivers was in demand as a lecturer and his influence and standing were considerable. And all the time his collection continued to grow. Indeed he felt a considerable urgency about collecting, recognizing that 'in a few years all the most barbarous races will have disappeared from the earth or will have ceased to preserve their native crafts'. It never seemed to have occurred to him that he might travel himself in order to collect, although he would do so in pursuit of his archaeological interests.

It became generally agreed that there was, in Pitt Rivers' own words, a need to establish a 'great National Anthropological Collection' and it was undoubtedly with this in mind that he arranged a loan exhibition of his

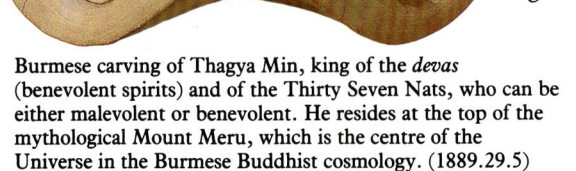

Burmese carving of Thagya Min, king of the *devas* (benevolent spirits) and of the Thirty Seven Nats, who can be either malevolent or benevolent. He resides at the top of the mythological Mount Meru, which is the centre of the Universe in the Burmese Buddhist cosmology. (1889.29.5)

4

material at the Bethnal Green branch of the South Kensington Museum (now the Victoria and Albert Museum) in the summer of 1874. It is clear from his speech at the opening that he had already seen the disadvantages of purely typological display and thought that if the National Collection ever came into being, it should also have geographical displays, for 'different points of interest' would be 'brought to light by each'.

He must have been an infuriating donor, reserving the right to add pieces, or remove them, as he wished. The museum's Curator was expected merely to arrange them as required. The inventory of the collection at this time shows that it was divided in four sections: 'skulls and hair', 'weapons', 'miscellaneous arts of modern savages including navigation' and the 'prehistoric series'. By 1878, the collection had outgrown the space available and was moved to South Kensington; it was becoming obvious that it could no longer remain a 'private collection on public exhibition'.

The turning point came in 1880, when the last of twelve heirs between Pitt Rivers and the considerable estates at Cranborne died. He decided to offer his collection to the nation for display at the South Kensington Museum, but this was refused on the grounds that, as the material was ethnological, it properly belonged with the British Museum collections.

Finally, through the mediation of various friends, Pitt Rivers opened negotiations with the University of Oxford and two years later, in 1884, the gift was accepted. Although he continued, particularly at first, to grumble and interfere and seemed convinced that he had made a poor choice, in fact his interests had already moved away from this first collection and his archaeological work was to be the focus of his attention for the rest of his life.

His new estates at Cranborne Chase were rich in archaeological sites, ranging from Neolithic and Bronze Age to Romano-British and later. Pitt Rivers excavated them with his usual energy and enthusiasm, producing scale models (which can still be seen in the Salisbury and South Wiltshire Museum) and detailed plans showing where finds had been made. He was also generous in making information available to fellow archaeologists, privately publishing lavish volumes on his work.

Pitt Rivers has been called the 'father of scientific archaeology', who transformed 'the pleasant hobby of barrow-digging to an arduous scientific pursuit'. His aim was not to unearth 'treasures' but to

Figure of a deity from China, possibly Fan Kwan, Judge of the Dead. In 1889, there were complaints to the Bishop of Oxford about displaying such 'heathen gods' in the same case as a Christian crucifix. (1884.59.108 : original Pitt Rivers collection)

Screens like this from Kalabari in the Niger Delta, Nigeria, formed the main feature of the household ancestral shrine. The spirits of the ancestors were thought to enter the figures and receive the sacrifice and prayers of their descendants. (1916.45.184)

General Pitt Rivers' medalet. These were designed for him to be buried when his excavations were infilled, in order, as he said, 'to show future explorers that I have been there.'

the initial list; Pitt Rivers had to visit them all, record them and add to the list. By the end of his life, he had set up a national programme of registration and protection.

He was in poor health during his last years and died on 4th May 1900. His achievements in a number of areas were to have far-reaching effects and it is perhaps only now that his considerable, if eccentric, contribution can be properly assessed.

recover as much information as possible; he recognised the importance of pottery sherds and animal bones in revealing the life of the people who used them. He also carried out practical experiments with flint knapping, digging with antler tools and throwing boomerangs. It was not until Sir Mortimer Wheeler, a disciple of his methods, began work in the 1930s that his pioneering contribution was really appreciated or understood.

As well as using the agricultural work-force as digging labour at the excavations once the harvest was in, Pitt Rivers provided for their education and entertainment by opening another museum at Farnham, with anthropology and social history as well as archaeological objects from his digs, providing an art gallery and the Larmer Pleasure Grounds. Here, exotic animals, an open-air theatre, a bandstand, Indian houses and much more, attracted visitors from a distance as well. It seems remarkably like a modern safari park, although in Pitt Rivers' view these free amenities were designed to educate the 'masses' and allow society to evolve as it should, defeating what he saw as dangerous revolutionary tendencies.

His part in what is now called 'heritage preservation' should also be remembered: in 1883, Pitt Rivers became the first Inspector of Public Monuments. This was the direct result of legislation to transfer responsibility for the maintenance of public monuments to the government. There were fifty, including Stonehenge, Avebury and Uffington Castle, on

Bronze cat from Ancient Egypt, representing the goddess Bast, part of the General's original collection. (1884.58.79)

The Collections at Oxford

As so often with important events, the significance of the General's gift to Oxford was not initially recognised. In fact, it was to be a landmark in the serious study of anthropology as an academic discipline in this country and a considerable influence on its development in the museum context.

Pitt Rivers' first requirement was that someone should lecture on the subjects of the collection and Edward Burnett Tylor was appointed in 1883 to a Readership in Anthropology. This was the first full-time position in anthropology in any British university and the Readership was converted to an *ad hominem* Professorship in 1895.

The deed of gift laid down that a new museum should be built to house the collections; an annexe to the University Museum. It was not only to be named after Pitt Rivers, but his name was to be inscribed on the entrance, both inside and out. You can see it there today.

Construction on the building began in the summer of 1885. It was the work of the Dublin-based architect T. N. Deane, whose father Thomas N. Deane had provided the basic designs for the University Museum. There were endless discussions about how to keep the costs down and the final result is sound, if inevitably pedestrian. The most interesting feature, architecturally, is the cast iron work which was very much a pioneering development of the time, as witnessed in the Crystal Palace and the great railway stations.

In accordance with the best evolutionary theory, the new museum was conceived as a logical extension of the natural history collections. The displays in the University Museum, which still show the evolution of *Homo sapiens*, were designed to lead to the study of humanity itself just next door. The collections were even initially put in the care of Henry Moseley, the Linacre Professor of Zoology. As he was also Professor of Comparative Anatomy and had made a private collection of ethnology when he was on the *Challenger* expedition to the Pacific, Moseley was well qualified for the position.

He also made two most fortunate decisions. One of his lecturers, Walter Baldwin Spencer, who was shortly afterwards to be appointed Professor of Zoology at the University of Melbourne, had the task of overseeing the packing of the Pitt Rivers material in South Kensington. Baldwin Spencer was to become celebrated as an anthropologist for his work on the Australian Aboriginal people. He maintained his links with the museum, and the archive holds some of his papers and photographs. One of Moseley's students, Henry Balfour, was asked to help with the unpacking when the collections arrived at Oxford. There could hardly have been a better choice. Balfour was to become the museum's first Curator in 1891.

The problem of the early years must have been truly daunting. The 15,000 objects in the founding collection arrived in Oxford before the completion of the building work and had to be stored in various scattered locations. Important new material was already being added from such donors as Heinrich Schliemann, E. H. Man and Arthur Evans; the university had also decided to bring together all the other material which properly belonged in the new ethnographic museum. This included the transfer of prehistoric material from the Department of Geology and such gems as the collection made in the South Pacific on

---

Professor Tylor transformed the look of the museum when, in 1901, he acquired the forty-foot Haida Totem Pole which dominates the Court. It is carved from one tree trunk, hollowed at the back so that it could be raised more easily into place. The bear, the raven, the frog and other creatures are all totems of the family to which it originally belonged in Masset Village, Queen Charlotte Islands, British Columbia. It was sold because there was no one who could rightfully inherit it and, after much discussion in the village, five of the nine hats of the Chief which were its topmost point, were allowed to remain in honour of Oxford University. (1901.39.1)

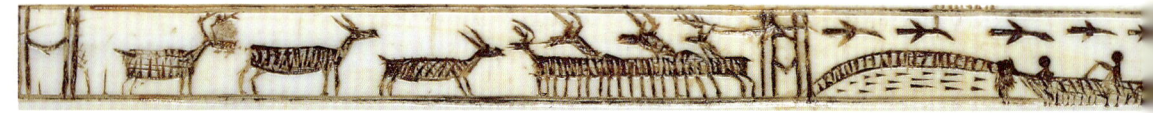

Walrus ivory bow drill used with a drill shaft, bit and mouthpiece, for working ivory. The carving shows scenes from daily life: caribou snares, birds flying overhead and men in a boat. From the Beechey collection, made in Alaska in 1826. (1886.1.693)

Captain Cook's second voyage in 1772–5 and the Beechey collection of Inuit artefacts from N.W. Alaska, made in 1826/7, from the Ashmolean Museum. There were some intriguing decisions: Tibetan bronze casting remained in the Ashmolean, but the African work came to the Pitt Rivers.

Not only had all this wealth of material to be organised, catalogued and put on display, but Balfour had to achieve this without any proper space in which to work on the collections, no such provision having been made in the original design. At first the Lower Gallery served as his office, design studio and workshop while the other sections of the displays were opened to the public as they were more or less completed. By 1888, the Upper Gallery was open in the afternoons, the Court followed in 1890 and finally the Lower Gallery in 1892. The staff at the time consisted of a Sub-curator, Balfour, with a salary of £200 per annum and two assistants, paid £1 and 15 shillings per week respectively.

Pitt Rivers himself was very unsympathetic to the problems and irritated both by the delays in opening and with Balfour, whose view of the collection he already suspected of diverging from his own. As he wrote crossly at the time:

'Oxford was not the place for (the collection) and I should never have sent it there had I not been ill at the time.'

The real problem was probably his loss of direct control – for the first time it was not his collection. Although he formally opened the museum in April 1891 he took little interest in it after that date.

Baldwin Spencer's eloquent photograph of a group of mourning Waramang women, Tennant Creek, Central Australia. (C1.17.14a, August 1901)

Right: A mourner's dress worn by the relatives of a deceased chief, made from bark cloth and pearl shells, with birds' feathers and discs of coconut shell. Part of the famous Forster collection, made in the South Pacific on Captain Cook's second voyage in 1772–5. (1886.1.1637b–1)

11

From the cases in the Lower Gallery – (*above*) various games, (*below*) jewellery.

The First Curator

Henry Balfour working on the weapons displays in the Upper Gallery in *c.* 1890.

Henry Balfour was just twenty-one in 1884 when he was asked by his Professor to help with the arrangement and installation of the Pitt Rivers collection in its new home. He had just graduated in zoology, had a particular interest in birds and orchids, rowed and fenced for his college, was a good classical scholar, a fine amateur musician and an accomplished draughtsman with an interest in all forms of art. No one could then have guessed that the Pitt Rivers Museum was likely to become his life's work.

It seems to have been tacitly assumed by the university that after the displays had been completed, no further provision for the museum need be made. There were endless battles in the early years, which have continued virtually throughout the museum's history, to improve the financial position and to establish a permanent staff, thus giving the museum the academic recognition it should have.

Balfour came from a wealthy family and he used his personal fortune for the museum's benefit; it financed his field work and allowed him to purchase widely for the collections. Without it, Balfour would not have been able to achieve all that he did and it exasperated him, to the point of threatening resignation, that the university would not recognise the museum's needs and make proper provision for them.

Balfour's training as a zoologist had taught him the skills of observing minutely and classifying material accurately, which he

Events recorded by the participants: a copy of a drawing from a southern African cave painting, showing the Sotho trying to rescue cattle from the San (1993.19.1), (*above*) and (*below*), Chukchi seal-skin painting brought back from the Bering Straits, Siberia, by the captain of an Arctic whaler in the early nineteenth century. The influence of Western contact can be seen in many of the scenes depicted. (1966.19.1)

hen applied to the collections in the museum. He was to develop an enormous range of interests, to which his publications bear witness; he wrote on subjects as diverse as the origins of decorative art, the natural history of the musical bow, primitive currency, fish hooks, West African brass casting and stone technology. He obviously had a particular interest in music and the musical instrument collections are one of the most notable of the Series which he built up.

Unlike the General he was a great traveller. He was usually accompanied by his wife, Edith, who was companion and research assistant, and his field trips included visits to Finland, Lapland, Assam (N.E. India), Kenya, Uganda and Nigeria. Wherever he was to go, Balfour collected for the museum. He also had a genius for getting other people involved in the search for specimens. A delightful series of letters, now in the museum archives, exchanged with Rudyard Kipling's father, the Curator of the museum at Lahore, reveal his charm and the warmth of the response he evoked.

The collections were always central to his work. He liked to teach in the museum itself among the objects and his enthusiasm was infectious, inspiring his students, many of whom were to join the Indian and Colonial Services, to collect for the museum in their turn. One

Photograph: John Reader.

Dolls and Combs from the Series in the Lower Gallery.

Photograph: John Reader.

15

Diploma student, Beatrice Blackwood, remembers him describing how one Sunday, working on the weaponry, he pricked himself with a poisoned arrow. Realizing that no help was at hand, he calmly sat with pencil and paper ready to describe his symptoms to the end. After about an hour, it became apparent that the poison was no longer lethal, but he told the story as a warning to take care.

This scientific approach underlines one of Balfour's greatest contributions to the museum: the meticulous documentation of the objects he acquired. To understand a material object one needs to know not only what it is, but how it was used and by whom and when and also how it was made. Only then can an artefact be set in context. Unusually for the time, Balfour seems always to have understood this and trained others to be equally rigorous. This background information is now one of the great strengths of the collections.

His obituary in the *Geographical Journal* in 1939 described him not only as a 'most loveable man, with a keen sense of humour' but also as 'an ideal museum man' of whom it was 'no exaggeration to say that he was the greatest authority on the material culture of primitive people in his day'. It is certain that without his influence, during the formative years of its development, the museum would not be what it is today.

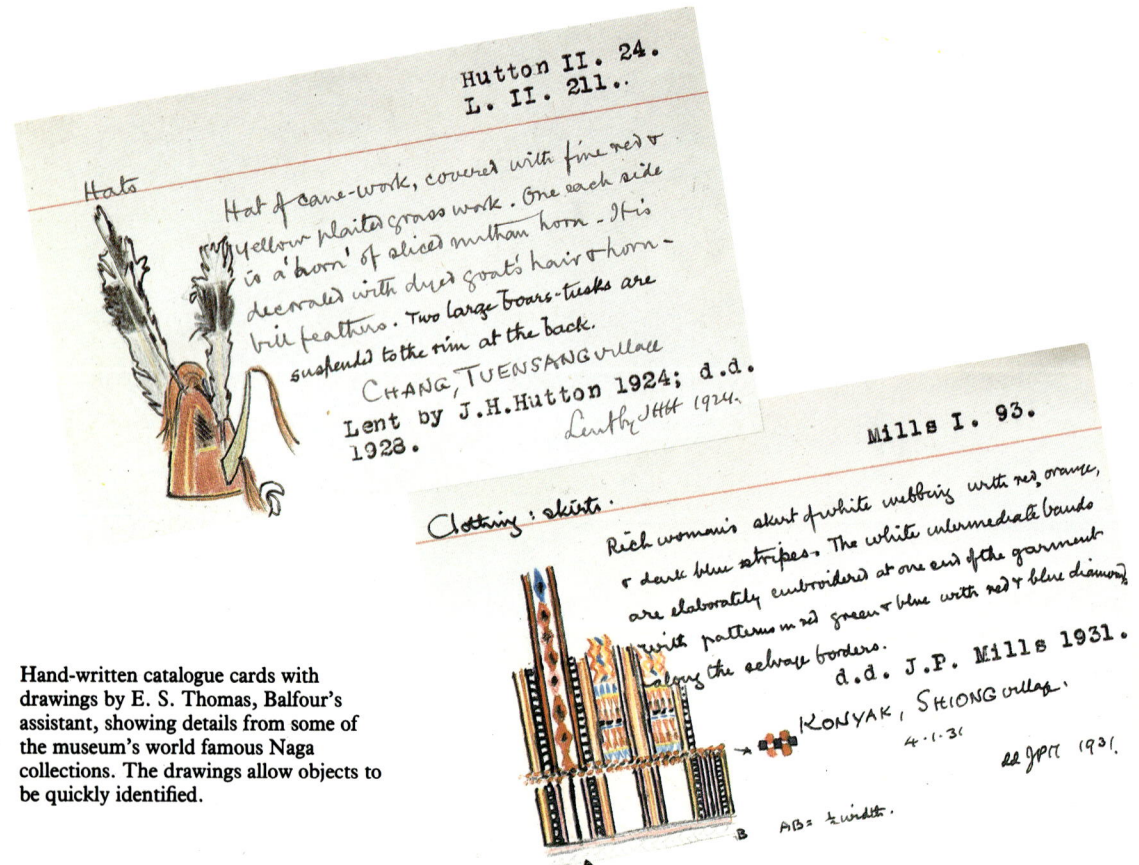

Hand-written catalogue cards with drawings by E. S. Thomas, Balfour's assistant, showing details from some of the museum's world famous Naga collections. The drawings allow objects to be quickly identified.

Nose flutes and photographs collected during Henry Balfour's curatorship.

Beatrice Blackwood

Beatrice Blackwood at Waylands Smithy in 1967 – one of the few photographs of her. (B66 A.63)

The third person who made an outstanding contribution to the development of the museum was Beatrice Blackwood. Diminutive, fearless and intellectually formidable, she was one of those extraordinary women who managed to break all conventional rules. Born in 1889 to the publishing family famous for creating *Blackwood's Magazine* in 1817, she had to put up a strenuous resistance to being 'finished' and taught only those accomplishments considered suitable for young ladies. In fact she won a scholarship to Oxford and graduated from Somerville in 1912, with a degree in English Language and Literature. She was then to work in a number of academic disciplines including anatomy and embryology, fitting in the Diploma in Anthropology and work with Abbé Breuil and the French prehistorians on the way. The Abbé described how she would be the first to enter a narrow or difficult cave in order to make sure that the bulkier male prehistorians could manage it. She also spent a good deal of time excavating Oxfordshire sites, often just ahead of the bulldozer, and in 1948 was to be elected a Fellow of the Society of Antiquaries.

Her field work, once she had transferred to the Pitt Rivers Museum as a Departmental Demonstrator, was to become legendary among anthropologists. She worked first in Canada and the United States, going to the Solomon Islands in 1929/30. Her own words from *Both Sides of the Buka Passage* give some idea of her approach and the level of acceptance she gained:

'To enlist the interested co-operation of the natives, it was sufficient to tell them that my people, who lived very far away, had sent me to see what kind of folk they were, what they did, and what sort of things they could make, saying that this was my work, just as their work was fishing and gardening, and that my tsunaun *(Chief) would be pleased if I could tell him all about them when I went home. This personal note particularly appealed to them, and they would sometimes say, in explaining something I had not properly understood: "We do not want you to tell your* tsunaun *anything about us that is not true." Note-book, typewriter and camera were accepted without question as aids to my work, the two latter arousing great interest.*

After I had been resident among them for a while, they began to come and tell me when anything special was going to take place in case I wished to be present. When a feast was held I was always invited, and they were delighted when, under the sponsorship of the women, I took part in their dances. During my morning

Sally the kitten 'among the headhunters.' (BB.P.11.1004)

Photograph: Beatrice Blackwood.

stroll around the village I was sure to be asked to join in some one or other of the day's activities, an invitation which I frequently accepted, gaining thereby a practical acquaintance with their methods of hunting, fishing and gardening, etc. . . . That they accepted me as a member of the community they showed when, on my return from a journey, they performed the appropriate ceremony for me as they would for one of themselves under like circumstances, and clinched it by saying: "Now you really belong to us." '

She records that while the men treated her as a sort of honorary man, allowing her to handle magical objects such as the bull roarer which would normally be kept from women, the women equally accepted her presence at purely female events.

Her next field trip to New Guinea in 1936/7 was potentially extremely dangerous. She had decided to go among the Kukukuku, who were head hunters, inhabiting an unadministered area of New Guinea visited only by armed soldiers. Undaunted, she set out with an alleged interpreter who actually only knew three English words and those 'bad ones but amiably spoken', a ball of wool and a kitten named Sally in a string bag. Sally's antics enchanted the warriors, many of whom came long distances just to see the little animal playing with the wool. They brought with them all sorts of artefacts to trade and Beatrice Blackwood made a remarkable collection for the museum. She was awarded the Rivers' Memorial Medal of the Royal Anthropological Institute in 1943 for her exemplary field work.

It seems typical that in the dark days of the Second World War, Beatrice Blackwood and Tom Penniman, the museum's second Curator, settled down to create the typewritten card catalogues of the collections which are still being used today. The thesaurus she created for analysing and categorising ethnographic objects has become a model for other museums and the basis of the Pitt Rivers' computerization programme. Miss Blackwood formally retired in 1959 and came to work the next day as if nothing had changed; she was working on the card catalogue up to the day before her death in 1975. She was a truly remarkable lady.

The museum Court.

The Textile Displays

The Museum Today

The Pitt Rivers Museum today evokes a variety of responses. It is 'a museum of museums' lost in a time warp. It should never be changed. It is a monument to colonialism filled with loot properly belonging to other people. It is a de-contextualized jumble. It is a glorious treasure trove of the unexpected, the beautiful and the intriguing. All these statements might be said to be true, though none represents the whole truth.

The Method of Display

The museum has retained much of its Victorian character. Painstaking labels hand-written by Henry Balfour can still be found attached to some of the artefacts and the 'feel' of many of the displays is quite different from those in more modern museums. The crammed black cases were initially devised almost as visible storage: the aim being to display as much material as possible for purposes of comparison.

In many museums the decisions about which objects should be displayed in isolation as important 'works of art' have already been taken for the visitor. Here the objects are on exhibition because they can reveal to us something about the culture of the people who made them. The things people use provide one of the most direct ways into their world. These objects are, of course, the products of art, in the deepest sense of being a revelation of human creativity. The most humdrum utensil can be an object of beauty because of the skill that went into its making. Sometimes this produces an amazing simplicity of design and sometimes intricate decoration quite unnecessary for its utilitarian purpose. There is a wonderful description by a Klickitat basketmaker of how the novice must go out into the woods and become one with the natural living world around her, then 'you can stitch your thoughts into your baskets'.

In Western culture, although the profound functions of art are recognised, it is seen as a thing in itself, which can be set apart from ordinary life. In non-industrial societies, its function is integral to the whole life of the people. Objects are made because they are part of the religious life, relating this realm to others, or placating the gods and ancestors; or they are part of the healing process in recovering from illness, or a means of understanding your own identity. They may be very ephemeral – made with infinite pains for a particular ceremony and not used thereafter; or they may be expressions of political status and rank, or of those individual choices all human beings make about decoration and personal adornment. The museum's Lower Gallery is full of these. Aesthetic qualities in the objects themselves and the skill of individual artists and makers are recognised and appreciated, but often as manifestations of spiritual power. An essential part of the museum's role in interpreting all this is to attempt not to make value judgements or decisions as to what is best and most beautiful. This leaves visitors free to make their own choices and responses.

The deed of gift laid down that the General's typological display should be retained unless the 'advance of knowledge' necessitated changes. For those used to ethnographic

Handmade pottery jar from Acoma Pueblo, New Mexico. Collected and donated by Beatrice Blackwood. (1928.9.1)

museums where the exhibits are arranged in geographical and cultural groupings, the displays in the Pitt Rivers Museum may indeed seem to divorce the objects from the context in which they are used. There will always be those who think that putting objects in cases is like 'stamp collecting', merely skimming the surface. However, the museum's temporary exhibitions provide a much needed opportunity to look at one subject or geographical area in more depth and to consider it in a wider contextual framework than is possible in the permanent displays. For instance, to celebrate the five hundredth anniversary of the discovery of America in 1492, the exhibition chosen was 'Basketmakers', which was an exploration of form and function in Native American baskets. Visitors also had the opportunity to see two Cherokee basketmakers at work, demonstrating how to handle different materials and discussing techniques and patterns. In such ways the museum finds itself once more at the forefront of material culture studies, just as it was, for quite different reasons, in its early days.

Although the Pitt Rivers has changed over the years it is still perceived as a Victorian museum. It has a curiously 'homely' quality which inspires considerable affection in those who know it. The underlying pattern of the displays may have been retained, but there has been an intellectual shift away from the General's theory that series of objects grouped together would reveal a steady progression in development. Now the artefacts are, for the most part, grouped together either according to their function, whether the use for which they were intended was practical, ceremonial, magical or religious, or according to the techniques used in making them.

The museum has been described as a demonstration of humanity's remarkable ability to solve the problems of life in differing cultures and environments. The study of the solutions which people find and their relationship to their environment is becoming central to modern general anthropology. The variety of the solutions and the juxtaposition of similarities and differences shown in the displays are part of the richness of the experience of visiting the museum. One can marvel at such things as the sheer ingenuity of making rainwear from walrus intestines, which can be seen in the Inuit display in the Court. One can also study particular techniques such as those involved in making pottery or weaving; or one can compare techniques, across cultural groups and at different periods of history. It was the General's contention that prehistory and ethnology were the past and the present of the same subject. Nowadays, of course, there is academic acceptance of the links between archaeology and anthropology and how each discipline can enhance the understanding of the other. This gives a quite modern dimension to what some may see as simply perpetuating a nineteenth-century approach to the displays.

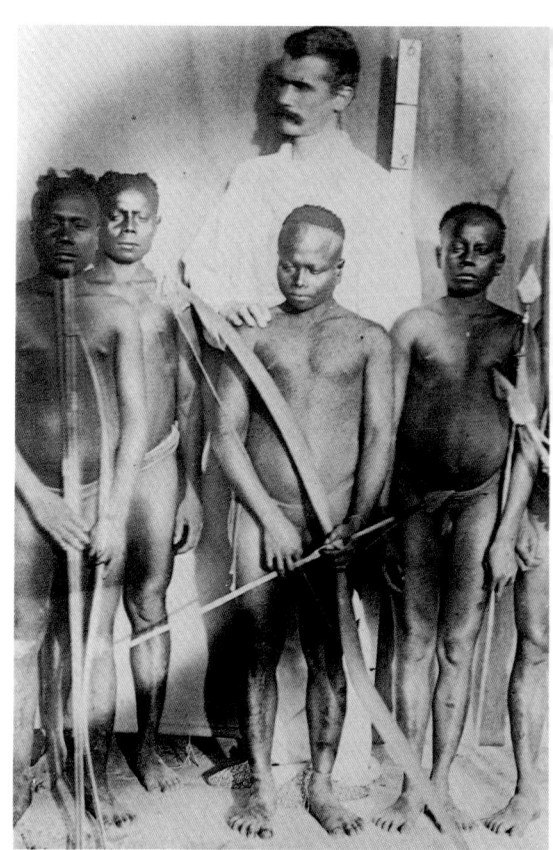

E. H. Man with a group of his 'Andamanese friends', c. 1878. (B30.5e)

How Material is Acquired

It is easy to forget how relatively small the founding collection was and how much material has been added since then. There are now probably about a million objects in the collections. They have come from a very wide variety of sources and, inevitably, many do represent Britain's colonial past. The field officers, missionaries and administrators who worked in far-flung parts of the empire naturally brought home reminders of the people whom they had governed and with whom they had lived. Some like, E. H. Man, had a sense of mission about recording culture before it vanished; he devoted his whole life to the people of the Andaman Islands with whom he worked. Others like J. H. Hutton and J. P. Mills in the Naga Hills collected over the years to illustrate the magnificence of the material culture of the area. The Hawaiian feathered chieftain's cloak was presented to the wife of Sir George Simpson, Governor in Chief of the Hudson Bay Company at the end of his tour of duty. Travellers like Mary Kingsley, T. E. Lawrence and Wilfred Thesiger have continued to give the museum objects and photographs which record their journeys. Archaeologists and anthropologists, both established scholars and research students, have made and continue to make collections in the course of their field work. This is the most valuable means of collecting today, because the artefacts come with detailed background material about their use and how they are made.

Artefacts are still purchased when funds permit. One of the most satisfying recent acquisitions was the traditional Greenland costume worn by Inuit girls for all important occasions. This was commissioned from Mrs. Haldora Davidsen, who spent more than a year on it to get all the details exactly right; she even sent to Iceland for the spotted seal skin demanded by tradition for the trousers, because those seals are now rare in Greenland.

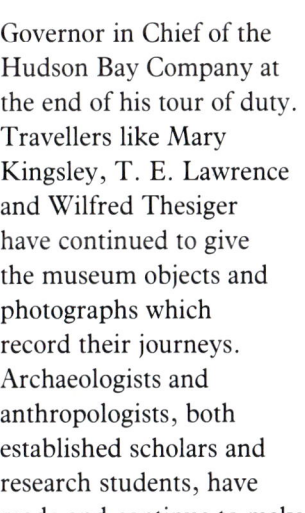

These two Yoruba carvings, one a caricature portrait of a District Officer, Mr. B. J. A. Matthews (1981.12.1), the other of a definitely unamused Queen Victoria (1965.10.1), show clearly how the Nigerians regarded the British.

Teenage girl's traditional dress from Sisimiut, western Greenland, commissioned for the museum. (1992.29.1.1–6)

25

Caring for the Collections

The museum's value as a resource of international standing has steadily increased over the years for a number of reasons. This is partly because it has a considerable amount of early, pre-contact material; that is to say, it was collected before it could be subject to outside cultural influences and Western ideas. It is partly because of the unusual strength of the archives: photographs were collected from the very beginning and always recognised as an essential component in understanding other environments and peoples and in recording 'our' relationship with them; while the sound archives have some of the earliest wax cylinder recordings ever made in the field. It is partly the strength of the documentation of the collections which makes it an information resource for other museums. (Unattributed material or vague general attributions are every curator's nightmare.) Maybe, above all, it is because of the early policy of collecting the 'ordinary and everyday' examples of objects. Just because they were ordinary, very few were preserved and so with the passing of time they have become rare and treasured, in some cases the sole surviving examples of their kind. The museum has, for instance, the only Fijian jew's harp in the world.

Ethnographic objects are by their very nature intensely vulnerable. They are often made of fragile, organic material which may not have been intended by its maker to last for any length of time.

Conservators would ideally keep everything out of sight in dark, environmentally controlled conditions, but that would defeat the object of the museum which is, of course, to make its collections available.

The artefacts themselves and the conditions in which they are kept have to be constantly monitored to ensure that light, temperature and humidity are controlled and that some insect population is not making a hearty meal of any of the collections. This is a constant battle, given the size of the problem, and skilled conservation is a vital component in the preservation of the collections for future generations.

Conservation Laboratory

The Ethics of Collecting

There are profound ambiguities in the study of anthropology and ethnography which any museum devoted to the subject must acknowledge. As General Pitt Rivers told the Anthropological Institute in his presidential address in 1876, '*Aborigines are dying out, or fast changing their customs; and even in civilised countries old landmarks are being removed so rapidly that in a few years the opportunity for collecting information will be lost . . . Many of the observations of travellers having been unscientifically made, or observed under the influence of foregone conclusions, are worse than useless.*'

That which is not recorded may be lost forever. The trouble is that, as the General said, those who record and observe bring their

Sixteenth or seventeenth century brass plaque from the palace of the Oba of Benin in southern Nigeria. Skilled use of sophisticated techniques reveals the high level of native craftsmanship. (1991.13.8)

The 'Nail Fetish' from Kakongo, Zaire, collected by the writer, Mary Kingsley. The figure, *Mavungu*, is studded with iron blades and nails, each one of which symbolizes a pact or legal agreement. Dire consequences were said to follow the breaking of one's word. (1900.39.70)

own cultural conditioning and inbuilt assumptions with them; it is extremely difficult, even now, when the problem is generally recognised, for anyone to be a truly impartial interpreter of the evidence.

Furthermore, as cultures come into contact, things change and this is a process which it is impossible to reverse or prevent, even if this were desirable. At the present time, when everyone is becoming increasingly aware of the fragility of traditional culture throughout the world, the pidgin English words spoken to Beatrice Blackwood by a Solomon islander in the 1930s, sound a real knell: 'White man he capsize altogether something belong before.'

The Pitt Rivers' collections are not only a record of Britain's colonial past and a historical repository preserving the culture of bygone ages – they equally reflect the results of cultural contact and try to include all the modern

27

Eighty years later: Tomokivona looking at his grandfather's photograph taken by Diamond Jenness in 1911. Photographed at Nikolo, Goodenough Island, June 1991.

Photograph: Michael Young.

adaptations and developments in styles and methods of production, such as African baskets made of colourful telephone wire, so that the record is an accurate one. The museum is also a rich source of material for those struggling to preserve what is being lost and repossess their own past. It has an active policy of working with indigenous groups whenever possible. For instance, experienced Maori weavers have come to study the techniques used in the Maori cloaks in the collection, while a Curator from the museum went to the United States to work with Native American basketmakers and learn from them at first hand. The Photographic Archive is involved in a field work project, using photographs taken in 1911/12, with the people of Goodenough Island, off Papua New Guinea, exploring different ways of looking at the historical record. In such ways the museum is actively seeking to explore common histories, which have many perspectives.

Of course, sensitivity to what is collected and, indeed, what is publicly displayed has changed considerably since the 1880s. Nowadays, for instance, at the request of Maori visitors, the Maori tattooed heads have been taken off display and other skeletal material, not properly held by this museum, has been returned via the Australian High Commission to the Aboriginal groups from whom it came.

And yet the 'other', the 'different' in particular perhaps many of the dark and ghoulish manifestations of humanity, such as shrunken heads and skull racks, remain on display to challenge us. One of the important functions of the museum is to teach us more about the human condition and our own humanity and to teach us to accept it on a much broader and more universal basis than that of our own limited cultural experience.

Who Uses the Collections

Many of those who visit the museum will be unaware that it is also a teaching department of the University. Oxford Anthropology was born in the Pitt Rivers Museum and, although it was later to branch into three disciplines: Cultural, Social and Biological Anthropology,

The first Diploma students in Anthropology, with Henry Balfour, in 1908, on the occasion of their practical examination in the Upper Gallery of the museum.
From left to right: Sir Francis Knowles, Balfour, Barbara Freire-Marecco, and A. Harley. (B66.3)

hese are now re-united in a joint School. The year 1992 saw the first undergraduate intake for the Honours' Degree in Anthropology and Archaeology. It has taken a hundred years to achieve this ambition. The museum also continues to have postgraduate doctoral students and those studying for the Master of Studies in Anthropology and Museum Ethnography. The use of the collections in teaching is still a high priority.

In 1911 the Lord Mayor of Oxford asked Henry Balfour if he would consider showing parties of schoolchildren round the exhibits in the mornings. This tradition has always continued and now there is a flourishing Education Service which offers help and advice to the thousands of school visitors who come each year, and collaborates in various outreach activities in the local area. The museum is a named resource for the National Curriculum.

Research enquiries on the object collections, the photographic, manuscript and sound archives cover an enormous range. Queries vary from: 'We are a class of ten-year-olds, doing a project on the Aztecs, please can you send us some information', to scholarly attributions of particular pieces.

But the museum is not only a scholarly resource. Artists and craftspeople have long found the collections a source of inspiration. A more recent development, arising from this, has been the active exploration of the relationship between the artist and the museum. This has led not only to workshops and schools' projects, but some major exhibitions of interpretative art in the museum, set among the permanent collections, attracting artists such as Kate Davis, Brian Catling, Chris Dorsett and Elizabeth Rosser. Their installations challenge our accepted ways of looking at things and encourage the finding of new perspectives on familiar material.

Above all the museum is, as the General originally intended, a place for everyone who wants just to enjoy looking at the objects and thinking about the human beings who made them.

Photograph: John Reader.

Ancient Peruvian workbasket, containing spindles, balls of yarn and raw cotton. (1952.7.89)

The Balfour Building

In the 1970s a magnificent new museum was designed by Nervi, Powell and Moya to be built on the Banbury Road. It was a daring and exciting conception based on an idea put forward by the General of a rotunda with concentric circles working outwards from the prehistoric material. Yet because it would have meant abandoning the old museum, one cannot but be glad that it never came into being. However, new galleries have been built on the Banbury Road site and there is room for much-needed further expansion when sufficient funds materialize.

Balfour Building: Music makers gallery with Metalworks' gamelan in foreground.

Henry Balfour, the first Curator, who built up the musical instrument collections, always hoped that there could be a 'whole room for music' and so it is fitting that the bequest from his only son, Lewis, in 1974, went towards achieving this. The Balfour Building, as it is called, opened in 1986. One of the galleries is devoted to the display of musical instruments, drawn from the museum's remarkable comprehensive collections. These include everything from conch-shell trumpets and paleolithic bone whistles to sixteenth-century virginals, nineteenth-century musical boxes, twentieth-century street pianos and Chinese fiddles.

Musical instruments must, of necessity, remain silent if they are to be preserved, but recordings of the music they produce can instantly bring them to life again. There is a sound system for the Music Gallery which does just this and also changing audio-visual displays.

The other new gallery has an exhibition of hunter-gatherer peoples, past and present. This combines the museum's traditional approach with modern thinking on the subject, mixing ethnology and prehistory, typological and geographical displays. It also allows the general public to see something of the important archaeological collections.

The museum that never was.

Design for new museum and Centre for the Study of Anthropology and Human Environment by Pier Luigi Nervi and Powell & Moya

Huli dancers from Papua New Guinea in the garden of the Balfour Building.

Photograph: Hélène La Rue.

The Balfour Building was conceived as a space in which things happen. It has witnessed children making masks, dancers from Papua New Guinea, adults learning to play hand bells, and singers from Africa, in addition to more conventional concerts and workshops. It is also the venue for a changing programme of small temporary exhibitions and for selling exhibitions by contemporary artists, photographers and craftspeople.

Musicians from Senegal and the Cameroons in the Oxfordshire Music Festival of Traditional Music in 1989.

Photograph: Hélène La Rue.

In Conclusion

Like most museums today, the Pitt Rivers is fund raising. It still needs more staff to care for its magnificent collections and, as anyone who visits the museum will be aware, suffers from an acute lack of space. The problem afflicts storage, conservation, the archives, even the offices. The university has set aside an area on the Banbury Road, beside the Balfour Building, where new galleries, and reserve collection storage, a joint anthropology library and more up-to-date facilities for teaching and research activities can be built. The plans are already in being; all that is needed is the finance. However, this does not mean that the main collections will be moved from the present museum.

Since that idea was even suggested in the 1970s, it has worried those who know the museum, as if they recognised that to dismantle what is here would be to destroy the identity of the place. It is almost as if the spirit of the collections and the objects and the cultures they reveal had fused into a unique entity. Some of the lines from James Fenton's poem about the museum perfectly capture its atmosphere, the blend of the strange and the familiar, the humdrum and the exotic:

Entering
You will find yourself in a climate of nut castanets,
A musical whip
From the Torres Straits, from Mirzapur a sistrum
Called Jumka, 'used by aboriginal
Tribes to attract small game
On dark nights', a mute violin,
Whistling arrows, coolie cigarettes
And a mask of Saagga, the Devil Doctor,
The eyelids worked by strings.

• • • •

Beware.
You are entering the climate of a foreign logic
And are cursed by the hair
Of a witch, earth from the grave of a man
Killed by a tiger and a woman who died
In childbirth, 2 leaves from the tree
Azumü, which withers quickly, a nettle-leaf,
A leaf from the swiftly deciduous 'Flame of the
Forest' and a piece of a giant taro,
A strong irritant if eaten.

• • • •

Yes
You have come upon the fabled lands where myths
Go when they die.

Nō masks from Japan.

• • • •

For those who respond to it, the museum speaks for itself, weaving its own spell and working its own special magic.